8.50
/ EC

AN ARMADA OF THIRTY WHALES

Volume 51 of the
Yale Series of Younger Poets
edited by W. H. AUDEN

AMS PRESS
NEW YORK

New Haven:

Yale University Press

London:

Geoffrey Cumberlege:

Oxford University Press

1954

AN ARMADA

OF THIRTY WHALES

by DANIEL G. HOFFMAN

WITH A FOREWORD BY W. H. AUDEN

Copyright © 1954, reprinted by arrangement with the author

Reprinted from the edition of 1954, New Haven
First AMS EDITION published 1971
Manufactured in the United States of America

PS
3515
O2416
A8
1971

International Standard Book Number:
 Complete Set: 0-404-53800-2
 Volume 51: 0-404-53851-7

Library of Congress Card Catalog Book Number: 73-144757

AMS PRESS, INC.
NEW YORK, N.Y. 10003

FOR ELIZABETH

Foreword

Reading Mr. Hoffman's poems, I find myself asking a very silly question: "Is there going to be a revival of 'Nature' poetry and, if so, how will it differ from nature poetry in the past?" It is significant, I think, that until quite recently nobody would have dreamed of asking such a question but that now, silly though I know it to be, I cannot help asking it.

It has always been difficult to write well, but, in a technological civilization, it is becoming increasingly difficult, in addition, to find themes worth writing about. One of the principal functions of poetry—of all the arts, for that matter—is the preservation and renewal of natural piety toward every kind of created excellence, toward the great creatures like the sun, moon, and earth on which our lives depend, toward the brave warrior, the wise man, the beautiful woman. Sometimes poetry regards the excellence of its subjects as self-derived, at other times as an outward and visible sign of an invisible uncreated Good, but in either case it is with the outward, concrete, and visible that it is concerned. Further, the subject of poetic celebration must possess at least two qualities, one of which is an invariable, power; it must, that is, be a real subject, a cause, not an effect. On the other hand, though poetry cannot praise weakness, it cannot praise pure force either. The Earth Mother may be mysterious and at times cruel in her dealings with men, but unless there were a pattern discernible in her ways, she could only be hated and defied; the Hero must be strong, but he also must be brave or magnanimous or wise; the Beloved must inspire, not simply enslave, if she is to be called beautiful.

Technology, by transferring power from nature to the social collectivity, has deprived power of a face and left all personal excellence without visible power. Even when the collectivity is beneficent, showering on us some unequivocal blessing like the refrigerator, poetry cannot thank it as it might thank a king who made wine flow in the streets; and when it does harm it cannot be attacked, for it is faceless and makes no conscious choices: in antiquity a tyrant could be satirized for his vices, but a modern dictator cannot really be praised or blamed, because he is an official or a medium rather than a person. Courage, wisdom, beauty continue, of course, to exist but, as it were, in private, and poetry finds it very difficult to communicate the excellence of anything that is not publicly visible. A writer today may believe, if he is a Christian like T. S. Eliot or Graham Greene, that the temporal world is an analogue of the eternal, or, if he is a platonist, that it is a parody, but it is very difficult for him to imagine what he believes, to portray, for instance a temporal relationship like marriage as anything but sordid and corrupting.

Further, the way of life which the machine imposes on us, replacing the rhythmical recurrences of Nature by mathematically identical "soulless" repetitions, has developed in us a horror of all recurrence and a corresponding obsession with novelty. The resistance of most people to poetry, the lack of interest displayed by many contemporary poets in the art of "numbers," is due, I believe, to their association of repeated pattern with all that is boring and disagreeable in their lives. Similarly, while novelty is a good—even the most traditional cultures have demanded that a work of art be in some sense "original" and not a mere copy—the idolatry of novelty is more destructive than any traditional idolatry and harder to cure. Tristan may be led to see that there is something excessive about his love for Isolde by being reminded that she will die; Don Giovanni cannot be cured in this way, because you cannot tell him that the supply of ladies will run out.

Still, Nature, however we may ignore or exploit her, is all about us, and, so long as we have bodies, however we may maltreat them, our relation to her has not been severed. The ever growing popularity of hunting, fishing, and mountain climbing are evidence of this but I am not sure that the experiences which such sports provide, precious though they may be, are, at least for poets, the most desirable. Insofar as they make the relation to Nature one of contest, the goal of which is human victory, and limit contacts with her to those of the greatest dramatic intensity, they may exacerbate rather than cure that unnatural craving for excess and novel thrills which is the characteristic urban disease. What is really needed is a much more modest, passive, and reverent kind of approach. One does not have to agree with all of his doctrines to think that Robert Graves' manual, *The White Goddess*, should be required reading for all poets.

A poet today, particularly perhaps if he is an American like Mr. Hoffman, who sets out to take his themes from Nature is in a very different and much more difficult situation than a Romantic poet like, say, Wordsworth. By the end of the eighteenth century the Newtonian cosmology had destroyed the ancient beliefs in Nature as the abode of actual spirits good or bad, so that the continued use in poetry of Greek mythology had degenerated into genteel periphrasis. At the same time, life was still rural enough for men to feel instinctively that Nature was numinous. Wordsworth's achievement in poetry, parallel to that of Kant in philosophy, was to preserve the validity of this feeling by describing it, not in the traditional mythological terms, but in terms of the psychology of his time. But the poet today is faced not only with the question of contemporary expression but also with the task of recovering the feeling which he and the public have largely lost, that Nature is numinous. He has to make a much more conscious and deliberate effort. At this point I hear the Accuser adopt his "honest Iago" voice: "This is sentimental rubbish. You don't feel that Nature is holy and as a modern man you never can. Genuine art is the mirror of genuine feelings, and the only real feelings you have are of self-pity at your alienation. So be frank, be modern. Express your pity for your self in the rhythmless language really used by metropolitan man." The only way to counter this lie is to realize its half-truth, namely, that our conception of Nature cannot be that of some prescientific magician, nor our modes of poetic expression those of some agricultural community without a written literature.

Mr. Hoffman has not been led astray by the Accuser. While admitting the pains and tragedies of life, he can find joy in life and say so. Nor, on the other hand, does he try to pretend to a Wordsworthian intimacy with Nature. He knows that, for any member of our urban culture, such intimacy is not given but is a prize slowly and patiently to be won: we all start as outsiders. Sometimes, as in "An Armada of Thirty Whales," he uses natural objects as heraldic symbols, but more often starts with direct observation and description. Such an approach produces, I feel, more interesting results. There is always a danger of becoming whimsical in using some animal as a symbol when you have no personal experience of it as an animal.

A number of Mr. Hoffman's poems are concerned with the same kind of place, the frontier between earth and water, and with the creatures associated with it, and they are written in the same kind of meter, a loose couplet, stopped between the lines and sometimes employing internal rhymes in lieu of end rhymes; e.g.:

> *All shrinks in the rage of the sun*
>   *save the courage of clams, and their faith:*
>
> *Sacrificing the water they breathe*
> *seems to urge the tall moon from her orbit;*
>
> *she tugs ocean, cubit by cubit*
> *over killdeer's kingdom*
>
> *and ends parched freedom.*
>   *Moon, with sky-arching shell*
>
> *and bright snout nine thousand miles long*
> *and anemones in her kelp hair*
>
> *that gleam in the heaven around her,*
>   *responds with the wave of their prayers*
>
> *or sucks the sea unawares.*
>
>   [THE CLAMS]

The skeptical caution of the last line seems to me right, but so does the analogy Mr. Hoffman perceives between the clams and human ritual. Indeed if such analogies are not valid, no art is possible. As Malcolm de Chazal has written: "Symbolism was born when Adam, wishing to tell Eve with a single gesture of the immensity of his love for her, pointed with his hand to the disk of the sun."

W. H. AUDEN

Contents

I

3   Incubus
4   The seals in Penobscot Bay
6   Winged Victory
8   In humbleness
9   An armada of thirty whales
10 Cape Breton
13 At Provincetown
14 Icarus, Icarus
16 Off Chichicastenengo
17 That the pear delights me now
19 Two propositions & an elegy
20 The larks
21 The clams
22 Old Bug up there

II

25 Auricle's oracle
26 On the extinction of a species
27 Lobsterpot labyrinths
28 Abstract: Contact
29 An antelope of canteloupe
30 É, the feasting Florentines
31 The voice of the woodthrush, played at half speed

III

35 X-rayed angels rib the sky
37 An age of fable
39 Dancing-Master of the pussycats
40 The flautist's breath turns reverie to sound
41 Ephemeridae
42 I brought my love a rose
43 I dreamt my love was but a child
44 I dreamt my love a-dying lay
45 Ode

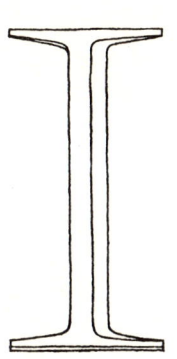

Incubus

What did the caterpillars do
last time the Phoenix died?
    They beat their breasts with a hundred fists
till one of them espied
the egg the ashes incubate.
Then, sure that wings would flame again,
they broke their bread on a mulberry leaf
and out of himself each wove the sheath
from which he'll burst on flaming wings
    after the peace of a season's sleep,
    after the peace of a season's sleep.

What did the little children do
when Christ was last time crucified?
    Each hid beneath a mulberry wreath
and on one another spied.
For they were playing Prisoner's Base
and as the teams hid face to face
the only thing that mattered much
was which was caught and which would catch
    before the evening grew more dark,
    before the earth and air grew dark.

The seals in Penobscot Bay

hadn't heard of the atom bomb,
so I shouted a warning to them.

Our destroyer (on trial run) slid by
the rocks where they gamboled and played;

they must have misunderstood,
or perhaps not one of them heard

me over the engines and tides.
As I watched them over our wake

I saw their sleek skins in the sun
ripple, light-flecked, on the rock,

plunge, bubbling, into the brine,
and couple & laugh in the troughs

between the waves' whitecaps and froth.
Then the males clambered clumsily up

and lustily crowed like seacocks,
sure that their prowess held thrall

all the sharks, other seals, and seagulls.
And daintily flipped the females,

seawenches with musical tails;
each looked at the Atlantic as

though it were her looking-glass.
If my warning had ever been heard

it was sound none would now ever heed.
And I, while I watched those far seals,

tasted honey that buzzed in my ears
and saw, out to windward, the sails

of an obsolete ship with banked oars
that swept like two combs through the spray

And I wished for a vacuum of wax
to ward away all those strange sounds,

yet I envied the sweet agony
of him who was tied to the mast,

when the boom, when the boom, when the boom
of guns punched dark holes in the sky.

Winged Victory

I

Phidias stared, and stood appalled
as the Emperor defaced

his stone commemoration of
the victories in Thrace.

"I want your stone to promise love
on a couch of feathered wings."

The sculptor gazed upon the wreck:
Body, undefiled

by those impurities of hand or face
which might deter a victor's lust

for chiselled stone to yield
to his imperious embrace.

Phidias' foot scuffed in the dust,
stubbed her marble eye;

he watched her raised to a gilded throne.
On the plains beneath the Parthenon

in ceremonious single file
the gala soldiery deployed:

Each man knelt down, removed his skull,
and placed it on the hallowed pile.

Then out of the Temple, into the air,
creasing the vacant sky

the Goddess of Victory circled them.
Her wings and beak like bronze sheaves clanked

and her talons held Phidias' heart.

2

May human hatred unto those
Who take the armless bitch to bed,
Who suckle at her stony dugs
And slake their ravening tongues in blood,
Invoke such violence on their heads
That in that instantaneous change
From animal flesh to maggot-food
Their brains may momentarily seethe
With knowledge of evil, knowledge of good,
Their souls with all their lusting did
To mankind's possible miracle.

In humbleness

Neither malt nor Milton can
Explain to God the ways of Man:
Hobnailed troops have ever trod
Upon the flocks who know that God
Has a passion, plan, or mind,
Or that the Universe is kind.

Come flood, come war, come pestilence,
Come Man at last to Common Sense:
At last admit, in humbleness,
Whatever spire he dares erect
Of either faith or intellect
Can be but his sarcophagus;

Yet even in that iron tomb
Man stirs again, as in the womb:
Tunnels free, then, word by word,
Rebuilds, and is again interred.
Read this in the histories:
The newsbreak, or Thucydides.

An armada of thirty whales

(Galleons in sea-pomp) sails
over the emerald ocean.

The ceremonial motion
of their ponderous race is

given dandiacal graces
in the ballet of their geysers.

Eyes deep-set in whalebone vizors
have found a Floridian beach;

they leave their green world to fish.
Like the Pliocene midge, they declare

their element henceforth air.
What land they walk upon

becomes their Holy Land;
when these pilgrims have all found tongue

how their canticles shall be sung!
They nudge the beach with their noses,

eager for hedgerows and roses;
they raise their great snouts from the sea

and exulting gigantically
each trumpets a sousaphone wheeze

and stretches his finfitted knees.
But they who won't swim and can't stand

lie mired in mud and in sand,
And the sea and the wind and the worms

will contest the last will of the Sperms.

Cape Breton

There, there is a clearer air
that clothes the clouds
than any you have seen elsewhere;

the dust that hovers on the roads
across the roaring valleys moves
like genial daytime ghosts

over bearded reinsmen roving.
The firs are gnarled there, their tight whorls
beneath rich needles in the steep wind showing

despite the summer's benign warmth
that it takes courage in the storming winter
to grip this soil, and faith, and strength.

Valleys one's delight here are renewing,
and over every hill a valley dips
where goldenrod and freshets and the strong

rude grace of rock the ice has split
invite the eye and lure the roving eye
of broadwinged hawk down down to streak

birdward or rabbitward tempestuously.
Here, by beaches made of brambles and
shards of shale where somersaulty

streams spread clear cold waters under
hilltops hunched like shoulders spined with pines,
the village houses—wood worn silver—stand.

There is a style of living here that says
in the long barn backroof sloping to the ground,
in the frontal gable of the staunch farmhouses

that toward the road unblinking, forthright, gazes,
This life is hard but it's worth living.
Roads twist through forests where the logsled blazes

tributary roads, on forests giving.
Ride on, or walk; you are astonished
in a brutal wilderness believing

yourself to be to find schoolhouses
self-sufficient in the clearings
at the road's turn, each one bearing

a name: "MacLeod's School," or "The Widow
MacKenzie's School." Here education's
prized, here reading is a

possession. If you've ever met one
of these Highlanders who found a Highland
far friendlier than Scotland,

if he's ever taken
your stranger's hand in his strong friendly hand,
you've found a use for contentment.

   This land makes strong men stronger. His
behemoth Barnum found here: Angus MacAskill,
whose wrists were thick as fir trees, yet 'H E W A S

A L O V E L Y   G I A N T.' What folk in the world have
   a hero so gentle?
Seeing themselves as a part of nature,
knowing their powers and the limits of their powers,

filling their backsloped barnrooves through the long hot
    summer
full of grain and lumber and rich hay for fodder,
they lay up against the cold grip, relentless,

of months like epochs when the world's frozen
and one might as well sit at the loom making an endless
tartan of thistles and rainbows and good wool woven,

while ice splits and the hawks scream and streams jangle
down down the glass valleys, till the winds wildly roving
blow winter away,
                      and the clear air grows warmer.

At Provincetown

Over the wharves at Provincetown
we watched the hooded gulls manoeuvre.

As one last gull, in late arrival,
flung his wings before our face

crying *"Wait!,"* . . . *"Wait!,"* in a race
to ride their aerial carousel,

we saw his dark-dipt head, eye-bead,
each individual grace recede

as all swooped up, then spun, and fell
unmoving in motion. Here was pure flight,
free from all bird-appetite.

Then the highest soarer saw
the *Mary Magdalena* yaw
laden low with mackerel.

      *   *   *

Beauty is the moment moving
toward unpremeditate perfection.

Over the wharves at Provincetown
the gulls within our arteries soaring

almost complete the great mobile
that all but froze gullsblood to steel.

Other wings across the harbour
flash like swords and dive for garbage.

Icarus, Icarus,

        —(I've watched the preening
seagull's sudden leap from the pier's pile,

seen his elbows clap a cloud, careening
artlessly around the rocking steel

bell buoy. Cling, dong: monotonously
swivelled between the same unchanging waves

articulating rootedness. The sea
holds hungry stone. Tempestuously

the porpoise leaps, leaps, spreads his frantic fin
but snoutward underwater rippling falls—

On the rockledge, I feel my own back arching.
    An old beachcomber strolls in ragged sneakers

and faded denim pants halfpatched. His folly
is the sluggish village's diversion: acres

on the hill he lets run all to yarrow
while he caresses cast-off seagulls' feathers.

I think I know why his shrewd slant squint follows
invisible fulcrums where the tern teeters,

    and why the little boy in his Mighty Mouse suit
spread his arms and leapt from that high rock

—in the pure power of intensest wish he put
all faith—dying, he affirmed it, saying

"I flied, for a minute, just before I fell")
    —what ecstasy of pride it was that shook

you loose from all that beeswax & those quills,
O how you soared, that instant before Breughel

showed human eyes unseeing at your fall.

Off Chichicastenengo

Off Chichicastenengo
I saw a green flamingo flying—

Bird-God of Guatemala,
leaf-winged, whose never-dying stems

were legs toe-rooted in
the sunlit air that nourished them.

And what delicious draughts
of light that out-thrust throat devoured

before bird-verdure soared
higher than eye could see or thought

could comprehend flamingo,
green, off Chichicastenengo.

That the pear delights me now

    That the pear's boughs
delight me now is
inconsequential.

But after fragrance come
bull bumblebees.
On ozone wings they hum,

on hairyhorny knees
rudely they enter,
nuzzle, gnash, & guzzle

nectar of the pear.
Roystering honeymakers,
wholly unaware

of the dust their bristles brought,
of the lovestrong draught
they pour down those pear-pistils.

    It's June now, and the petals
have dropped, dried, crumbled,
in dust they've blown away.

Bees snarl in thick thistles;
pearboughs, hung in the hot day,
sprout green nubs now. Birdcalls

drench the leaves like fragrance;
fruit grows opulent in
summer lightning, heat, rains.

Sensuous the pears hang
richly, sweet and bursting.
Pears plop down. Birds follow, thirsting.

    Nights nip the earthskin tighter,
sap stops of a morning,
sunred leaves more harshly flutter;

old pears the starling pecked at
wrinkle in the waning shade.
Fruit sourly lies, rejected

till it's out of the earth invaded:
maggots rapaciously & noiseless
fatten on fermented juices

and the gristle wriggles through
their sniggling tails & slime
spreads beneath the peartree.

    Some squush remains, though,
some meat around the seed.
When Indian Summer strains

the last warmth through the orchard
pearpits feast and feed
and stir, & burst, & breed:

Earthward plunge the tendrils.
    That the pear delighted me
is wholly incidental,

for the flower was for the fruit,
the fruit is for the seed.

Two propositions & an elegy

Toil is death in action where
flesh is not moved by soul's intention,

yet complichorded gadfly-nerves
cannot long sustain the fiction

of a sensuality
where flesh, by being absent, glories.

A wreath: for all who dream, self-wrong'd,
of cabbage worlds made out of words

where paradisal bugs & birds
chirp disembodied silent songs.

The larks

An exaltation of larks arising
With elocutionary tongue
Embellish sound on morning air
Already fringed with scent of dung;
The curate in his curacy
Hearkens to that natural song,
And maids like wood-doves in their purity
Rise to matins' golden dong.
Their prayers are sweet high exultations
Whereon untrammeled spirits wend,
Forgetting flesh and breakfast. Under
The rectory eaves, the larks descend.

The clams

    In the Bay of Fundy the clams
lie stranded, half-dry, by the tides

forty feet higher than sea
in killdeer's kingdom.

    Underground, they erect valved snouts.
Wet freckles sprout over the beach:

Each trickles a droplet, and each
attests to the desperate hope

that attends each ritual drop.
    Lie ten-hours-buried in sand

and the swirl of salt and the wet
seems an Age before suffering began.

All shrinks in the rage of the sun
    save the courage of clams, and their faith:

Sacrificing the water they breathe
seems to urge the tall moon from her orbit;

she tugs ocean, cubit by cubit
over killdeer's kingdom

and ends parched freedom.
    Moon, with sky-arching shell

and bright snout nine thousand miles long
and anemones in her kelp hair

that gleam in the heaven around her,
    responds with the wave of their prayers

or sucks the sea unawares.

Old Bug up there

On Faneuil Hall there squats a copper
more-than-man-sized green grasshopper.

Impaled above the Farmers' Market,
snow-slow smoke and sleet have darkened

him. His mandibles munch the seedless wind.
No hunger's his, no brass caresses;

he leaps the rooftops toward no granary.
Lashed by acerb winds he spins

to point the way. But men are heedless.
    Old Bug, you remind me of someone,

like you above a city raised
to seem far larger than alive.

You're not the only one that's placed
on such an eminence. And if

fewer follow your globe-eyed gaze now
than when this harbour was spined with masts,

I'll tell you bluntly, you're not first
nor last to point out true unfollowed ways.

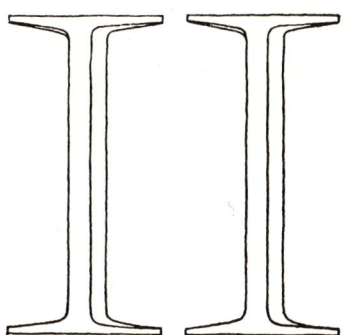

Auricle's oracle

Intensity, when greatest, may
Prove ludicrously small.
Who concentrates compellingly
More than the snoutish snail,
Hauling gunless turret up
Perpendicular glass,
> By muscle of mind and bodily ooze advancing,
> Atop at last the aquarium glass balancing?

Yet passion at its most intense
Consumes the minuscule.
The focus of the spirit's lens
On whatever the self may will
Like sunlight squeezed through a reading-glass
Turns trash to flame. The ooze congeals
> In a golden signature of snail-identity,
> Etched in glass by the snail's and the sun's intensity.

On the extinction of a species

Avast, the Pileated Woodpecker:
Square-hole-knocker in the pine,
Wears his ivory tower as hatchetnose
Crested with a wedge of flame,
& busily bangs his wooden signature.

Death drops more birds than birds drop eggs
—Promethean feathers on suburban hills
Are rare. But those square holes
(Dark images) in a living frame
Endure , endure , endure , endure .

Lobsterpot labyrinths

    Lobsterpot labyrinths wait. A porridge
of sand dries slowly. Sunlight in cages
and tides that seep below the cordage

have some connection with their waiting.
Ternmewed winds pour past their ribs
gathering old fishheads gaping

with the smell of death; there is a splendour
in their ramshackle spined ridgepoles
structural as architecture.

But drop one where the current yaws
unlit, its ramp wrought miniature
tensing to tread of knuckled claws

that probe the cordage aperture:
Primordial patterns close like doors
upon the crusted Minotaur.

    That's what lobsterpots are for;
yet traps hold pleasure free, abstract.
Did Daedalus need a beast to spur

artist to art or artifact?

Abstract : Contact

Boys in classrooms press the points
Of compasses upon their pads

Till line returns upon itself
As the fabled hoopsnake bites its tail,

Enclosing all the mysteries
Of Euclidean Plane Geometries.

Boys on the crossbridge dangle down
Their feet till water's at toe-tip;

Drop pebbles; watch inverted clouds
Rocked on rings, though Heaven's still.

Diligent draughtsmen, shoeless truants:
Scholars of the circle's nuance.

An antelope of canteloupe

inhabits the mind
of the man on the raft. He
should pray for rainwater
yet fondles in his brain
the rough red quartered rind
of a fresh cut ripe melon,
a rockinghorse melon
that mounts a sleek hind.

A marriage of mirage

and desperate truth
showers parched seams of
his soul with brainwater,
though the sky spews no rain.
His whistling cracked mouth
chomps on the roebuck,
incontinent roebuck
dripping in drouth.

É. the feasting Florentines

    stared, astonied all,
As the raging lion
    (archangelical!)
Adown the table where they sate
    strode with golden growl
That Michelangelo in butter
    carved, a spoon his trowel.

    Florentians, being men of sense,
when time melted their wonder
    Passed around the fresh tall staves
and ate them thick with butter.

The voice of the woodthrush, played at half speed,

   reveals to the halting ear
   the fullstopt organ that pours through floodgate reed
   such somersaults of sound like waters falling
   in dark crystal chambers
   on iron timbrels

   withholds from what we hear
   those haunting basses, loud but too deepkeyed.
   This slow bisected bird's yet wilder calling
   resounds on inward anvil:
   pain is mortal, mortal.

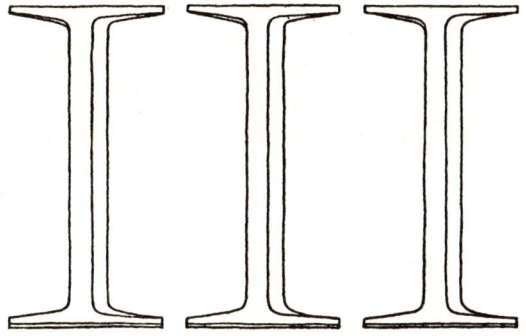

X-rayed angels rib the sky,

      X-rayed angels rib the sky.
Their structural luminosity

sheds visible glory on
the apple blossoms.

Black burgeoning boughs bend
in generosity,

shed effable flakes of colour and
odour, delighting

the hermit thrush. Migrating
mateward, he pauses silently, beholds

that skyswoopt silver & sweet air
trailed from angels stript of flesh

and then whirled upward by these things
in solitude he sings,
                he sings.

      Those ribs of angels hang like
shadows above the earth turned lately.

One feels the dark approaching in
the cage that bars the sun;

her eyes turn agate at the chill
of evening. Loneliness wraps round

her heart the burgeoning pain and she
wants to cry out but dares not cry

for in that silence with her eyes held
closed she can pretend

there is no death. O she cannot
believe that life could end . . . she hears

his call rejoice the appletree, and stares
past the inconsolable night.

    Anguish will not cease in appletime
nor music, though the evening falls.

An age of fable

Petit the Panther's come to town.

With great discrimination
He places on the rude concrete
His cushioned, grass-accustomed feet.

His motions are most musical:

In subtle tempi, baton-tail
Conducts a silent clawed quartette
As foot, foot, foot, & foot, step-step.

Panther prowls through telephone booth,

Highway, subway, chromium bistro,
Video trees, spikediron hedgerow,
Skeletal wires. All lack the couth

Ferocity of jungle growth,

Lack dignity of death & birth.
Goaded onward through the maze
By burning blood between his thighs

Or by some supernatural sense,

He leaps beyond all artifice:
Blots the sickly neon solstice,
Drops with graceful violence

Beside the beauty in her trance.

Beneath her leafy counterpane,
She stirs: Catfurs she disenchants!
Now Death's enchanted by their dance.

Dancing-Master of the pussycats

Dancing-Master of the pussycats
rapped his viol da gamba
& played a courtly air,

Played Buxtehude's minuets.
Who sees, beneath their bows, a samba
rippling under fur?

Who hears their padded castanets
or sees the light leap from their amber
eyes, may choose to stir

the natural graces of his pets;
Or choose the postures of the chamber
required by their Dancing-Master.

The flautist's breath turns reverie to sound,

The flautist's breath turns reverie to sound;
His hungering loneliness is music now.

Asnooze upon each other's breasts, the cottagers:
Half-harmonies they hear. Now each half-wakens,

The desolate skeletons of their selves lie bare,
The bonebox round each heart's a cage of longing.

Each beats alone and naked now. They hear
Woodnotes everywhere; and everywhere

The impenetrable hugeness of the dark,
Caught in the world's gizzard, they turn toward

Each other's loneliness, till face to face
A triumphant and companionable chord

—Coda to the flautist's monody—
They chaunt upon their fleshly instruments.

Ephemeridae

    Dark specks whirr like lint alive in the sunlight.
The sky above the birches is disturbed.

Swarms swarm between pure heaven and treetops:
it's the mayflies' four-hour frenzy before their fall.

Waterward, they lay eggs in their dying
spasms, having then endured it all.

    For five long shimmering afternoons that summer
we walked beneath the birchgroves on the shore

and watched the empty light on leaftips pour
and out of nowhere whirled the nebulae,

gadding gilded, all green energy, toward death.
    After, the birches stirred, and we beneath

saw south-flying mallards bleak the air.
Green turns husk now. The world's shrunk to the bone.

    Our thin flesh alone
through this long, cold, fruitless season

scampers frantic in wild whirligig motion
while larvae of the mayfly wait

and mallards migrate and the sap runs slow;
ours alone from time strains to purchase

    pleasures mayflies find among the birches.

I brought my love a rose

I brought my love a rose
a full blood red.
Anybody knows
what my heart said,
here my heart was heard,
here love, take this rose
to your porcelain bed,
here fragrance & the thorn
mingled until morning
odour, touch, word
blossomed, withered
to be reborn.

I dreamt my love was but a child

I dreamt my love was but a child.
Asleep, by water's edge, she smiled;
I saw her then to fullness grow
And in her hair the lilies blow
That once a wanton swan beguiled
In the Aegean long ago.

And then I saw the raging years
Shower her with silver spears
And where the flaming bird had pressed
Those great white wings, beneath her breast
An image grew too fond for tears
Asleep in that dark-watered nest.

I dreamt my love a-dying lay

while I beside her stood austere
to see my paradise decay;
From underneath the ground I heard
her tunnelled agony of despair
ricochet from earth to air;
I learned the word that Adam's ear
in Eden heard the day Man fell
(Who, tasting Mercy, swallowed Hell).
And then I saw Death lovingly
take his long fingers from the scythe
to gather ants & worms & me
from out the muck wherein we writhed.
He laid me where my coffin sits
and nailed the lid with cigarettes.
He wove a lily garland sweet
which insects crawled upon to eat.
Then he laid my coffin down
in the lonesome graveyard ground.
Down he laid my coffin, by
the bed wherein my saviour died.

Ode

1

When both our bodies in one whole
Were joined, their grubbing histories
& our lonely souls' imprisoned rant
Were swept immaterially aside:
Unbearable exaltation shared
That throbbing unity of the sun
Until with death of boy & girl
Subsiding in the dark cocoon
Cradled in your curving thighs
And your head on my crooked arm
We were, unknowing, all we'd done,
As infants sleep before they're born.

2

Some instant in that deep fond sleep
Nor felt, recorded, now unknown,
A seed was sown.
Deep in your warm down body's weal
Two cells commingled: A soul leapt
From God's eye forth, alive & tingling,
And all that while
We slept.

3

Three months about our daily labours,
Buying groceries, reading the papers.
Beneath the navel now a bulge burgeons.

A face lies there with sunless features;
If plunged from the womb, a book advises,
Into the terrifying brightness of the air

And placed then in a glass of water,
Would struggle feebly, simulating life.
This child not yet a child would surely die

Instinctively forfending death!
Three months about our daily labours:
Part way up the stairs, a pause for breath.

4

The year is half full swung now. We
Move more slowly than when last
Ripe apples pummelled the soft grass.

Who goes where we go? Who lives under
That anonymous mound? Our image
Through flickering centuries grows fuller

Past the pickerel, cygnet, hare,
Swims through sludge & stream & air
And wears the womb as atmosphere

And wears inviolable peace where there's no
Guilt nor knowledge and none's needed.
But your strength, your breath, your blood feed it.

5

Down green corridors of moan
Your voice tolled the spirit's pain.
Caught in the body's gripe, it wrung
Gnashes from that bravely muffled gong.
Your voice down greentiled aisles of pain
Piled agony on my tight breast bone.

But you suffered alone.

What monstrous mechanism did I begin
That rams apart your wrenching bone?
What natural force makes the winds scream
And the seas swell
And star-clappers in the heavens toll?
I seized your clenched fist
And closed those nails about my wrist;
Hands that passion could transmit
Were powerless to couple pain.
Alone you bore birth's harsh bruises.

Love puts our bodies to rude uses.

6

Nestle, darling, on your mother's breast;
Let fade birth's roar and the first breath's shrill alarm,
Drink in her warm white sweetness, strength, and rest

Cradled in the crook of her curved arm.
Hush a bye, my crying tiny one,
I'll exorcise your sleep from hovering harm

And shade you from the pitiless mortal sun.
There is no going back to that dark place
Where life is effortless and pain was none;

Passion, time, and accident will trace
From the pealing clouds of this loud cockscrow's dawn
A destiny upon your cherished face,

While Father and Mother love you, and look on.

Fledgeformed nurseling, infinitely small
Yet fashioned cunningly and wholly dear,
None could foretell how we should more than all

Love love you, lying helpless here.
Our own lost infancies on your cries croon,
In you our childish lineaments reappear

More delicate, perfected at the bone.
One little needs imagine lithe girlgrace
As will attend your casual movements soon;

Blossoming from our lonely souls' embrace
Mindmagic, heartwish, will, will be your own.
Yet we're your lineage, you are all our race—

Three-personed, by continual love made one.